# 1,000,000 Books

are available to read at

www.ForgottenBooks.com

Read online
Download PDF
Purchase in print

ISBN 978-0-266-13645-3
PIBN 10934900

This book is a reproduction of an important historical work. Forgotten Books uses state-of-the-art technology to digitally reconstruct the work, preserving the original format whilst repairing imperfections present in the aged copy. In rare cases, an imperfection in the original, such as a blemish or missing page, may be replicated in our edition. We do, however, repair the vast majority of imperfections successfully; any imperfections that remain are intentionally left to preserve the state of such historical works.

Forgotten Books is a registered trademark of FB &c Ltd.
Copyright © 2018 FB &c Ltd.
FB &c Ltd, Dalton House, 60 Windsor Avenue, London, SW19 2RR.
Company number 08720141. Registered in England and Wales.

For support please visit www.forgottenbooks.com

# 1 MONTH OF FREE READING

at

www.ForgottenBooks.com

By purchasing this book you are eligible for one month membership to ForgottenBooks.com, giving you unlimited access to our entire collection of over 1,000,000 titles via our web site and mobile apps.

To claim your free month visit:

www.forgottenbooks.com/free934900

\* Offer is valid for 45 days from date of purchase. Terms and conditions apply.

English
Français
Deutsche
Italiano
Español
Português

# www.forgottenbooks.com

**Mythology** Photography **Fiction**
Fishing Christianity **Art** Cooking
Essays Buddhism Freemasonry
Medicine **Biology** Music **Ancient Egypt** Evolution Carpentry Physics
Dance Geology **Mathematics** Fitness
Shakespeare **Folklore** Yoga Marketing
**Confidence** Immortality Biographies
Poetry **Psychology** Witchcraft
Electronics Chemistry History **Law**
Accounting **Philosophy** Anthropology
Alchemy Drama Quantum Mechanics
Atheism Sexual Health **Ancient History**
**Entrepreneurship** Languages Sport
Paleontology Needlework Islam
**Metaphysics** Investment Archaeology
Parenting Statistics Criminology
**Motivational**

OF THE

# HARMONIA SACRED MUSIC SOCIETY

## OF PHILADELPHIA,

WITH ITS

## CONSTITUTION AND BY-LAWS.

PHILADELPHIA:
CRISSY & MARKLEY, PRINTERS, GOLDSMITHS HALL, LIBRARY STREET.
1852.

OF THE

# HARMONIA SACRED MUSIC SOCIETY

OF PHILADELPHIA,

WITH ITS

## CONSTITUTION AND BY-LAWS.

PHILADELPHIA:
CRISSY & MARKLEY, PRINTERS, GOLDSMITHS HALL, LIBRARY STREET.
1852.

# OFFICERS

OF THE

# HARMONIA SACRED MUSIC SOCIETY.

PRESIDENT.

## W. H. W. DARLEY.

TREASURER.

## GEORGE F. JONES.

SECRETARY.

## WILLIAM A. ROLIN.

### BOARD OF DIRECTORS.

| | |
|---|---|
| W. H. W. DARLEY, | JOHN R. WELSH, |
| GEORGE F. JONES, | EDWARD C. KRUG, |
| WILLIAM A. ROLIN, | BRYANT FERGUSON, |
| GEORGE W. WOOD, | R. B. DAVIDSON, |
| THOMAS M. DAVIS, | ELI GRIFFITH, |
| BENJAMIN F. SCULL, | JOHN WELCH. |

# ADDRESS.

THE city of Philadelphia, with a population of nearly half a million, should possess at least one institution, expressly devoted to the cultivation and improvement of *Sacred Music.* That it does not, is one of those anomalies for which it is difficult to account. Music, in a general sense, is very extensively cultivated in our midst, and the assertion may be made without fear of contradiction, that the taste of the musical circles of Philadelphia is far more correct and refined than that of our sister cities of the Union. There are amateurs among us whose talent places them in an advanced position of the art. Many of them have given their attention to the higher descriptions of sacred music, and yet, notwithstanding strong exertions have been made to interest the public mind and taste in this particular branch of the science, it has proved almost fruitless. Some attention has of late years been given to the improvement of Church Music, but much remains to be done in that department. Shall the advantages so far gained, and the taste thus *partly* awakened, be of no avail, or shall we continue to strive with renewed effort, until the end be attained?

Repeated attempts have been made during the last thirty years, to establish Sacred Music societies in our city, but without success. They have been formed, and started into life, but after a short existence, have expired, and are now almost forgotten. It would be useless to enumerate them, or to narrate particularly the causes which have operated against their permanent establishment, but it is obvious to all who have given the subject their careful attention, that there have been radical defects in their *organization*, or the manner in which they have expected to carry on their operations. The want of success, however, is not altogether chargeable to those who have been the originators of the numerous associations referred to. Their efforts were laudable, and deserved a better fate than failure. Our citizens have stood aloof too much; they have not sympathized with the exertions which have been put forth: their taste in this department has not been reached, *awakened* and *fostered*, as it should be. The consequences, therefore, have been disastrous, and the struggle thus far, has been in vain. Properly appreciated, these considerations will be of great benefit to those of us "who come after," and great caution must be observed by all making similar attempts, to avoid the difficulties their predecessors contended with, and to remedy (if possible) the defects that have heretofore existed, either in organization or plan of action.

The HARMONIA SACRED MUSIO SOCIETY OF PHILADELPHIA was organized in the last quarter of the year 1850. From a small, but determined effort on the part of its original projectors, it has sprung into an existence which is now believed to be a vigorous and healthy *youth;* we hope to see it expand into the full stature and strength of *manhood*. That which has by many been justly considered a radical defect, the want of an act of incorporation, is, in the case of our society, obviated, for a charter has been obtained from the Legislature of Pennsylvania, liberal in its provisions, and sufficiently comprehensive in its details, to satisfy all who are interested in our welfare. One difficulty, therefore, in the way of a permanent establishment and probable success, has been removed. Another obstacle in the way of successful exertion, the absence of the desired taste for sacred music on the part of our citizens, is also being rapidly remedied, for the most indifferent observer cannot fail to see that the taste for music of every description has been increasing for several years past, and we are happy to say, to a very great extent. Besides, our citizens are not fully aware of the fact, that the "great masters" of every age, have given their loftiest efforts to the production of *sacred* music. Beethoven, Mozart, *Handel, Haydn, Rossini,* and hosts of others, have sent forth to the world the most exquisite, sublime and soul-stirring melodies and harmonies, bearing *sacred* sentiments, devoted to the worship, adoration and praise of the Almighty, the Creator, and the Father of us all.

Another difficulty in the way of success, has been the want of a *rallying point* of some magnitude, which is especially necessary to the welfare and proper establishment of a Sacred Music Society. The great expense of orchestral accompaniments in organizing, practising and performing, has been a serious weight upon the pecuniary resources of an association of this kind. Although not wishing to do away entirely with so desirable an accompaniment as a well balanced orchestra, it was proposed to have a large and powerful organ built, one that would produce grand orchestral effects, and every variety of beautiful combinations. A number of our citizens were waited upon, by a committee, and with commendable liberality they subscribed, in a short time, a sum sufficient to build *a noble instrument of the largest class,* which will be worth, when completed, about *seven thousand dollars.* The society issued certificates of loan to each subscriber, bearing interest from the date of payment, in shares of twenty dollars each, and a contract was immediately made, with Mr. J. C. B. Standbridge, of our own city, a gentleman well known among us, and one who has the ability and skill requisite to produce a splendid specimen of this most noble of all instruments. The result of his labors will be such as to leave no doubt that it will be considered the largest and best organ in the United States, and one of the "lions" of Philadelphia. It will contain about sixty stops, comprising about *three thousand pipes*, and the effect of this instrument, united with a well-drilled, efficient and powerful chorus, must certainly be not only grand, but pleasing to every lover of this soul-inspiring art.

Owing to the enterprise and public spirit of our townsman, Mr. George W. Watson, a splendid hall is being built, (in Chesnut street, between 12th and 13th streets,) in which the organ will be placed. Thus a "*rallying point*" is made, a *home* for our members is found, and with judicious management, and an untiring wish to please, we confidently expect success.

To those who join us, wishing to cultivate and improve their knowledge of singing, we offer the inducement of instruction and amusement at a very small expense, for each season, which is more than repaid them by the concert tickets given to each member. In addition to this, it is intended to give relief to such members as may require it in time of sickness and distress, as the charter expressly provides for this praiseworthy object, which provision can be extended as the means of the society may allow.

To those who become subscribers to our concerts, we shall give (to the best of our ability,) selections from the works of the *Great Masters*, which will be increased in great variety, as rapidly as the means of the society improve. It is proposed to give a series of concerts each season, to which a limited number of subscribers will be admitted on the same terms as is customary with other societies, adding the privilege of attending the rehearsals of the society at such times as the by-laws from time to time may provide.

The love of music is as yet only partially developed in this country. A *free* and *prosperous* people *must* love " the divine art." We believe the time to be rapidly approaching when the influence of music will not only be universally acknowledged, but universally *felt*. Our city has not kept pace with others of our country in its regard for sacred music, but we are beginning to awake to the importance of a full and universal cultivation of the taste for music of every kind, and when once aroused, we shall not soon return to our slumbers. So refining and so elevating an art, when once appreciated and enjoyed, will not be permitted to leave us, but it will be desired more and more, until *all* shall feel its power, and all enjoy its presence.

The art of Sacred Music is yet in its infancy, so far as the practice and love of it is concerned. Few are aware how susceptible of improvement is the performance of it. It must, it will have its proper place in the hearts of the lovers of music generally. " It has a power peculiarly its own; a purifying, ennobling and elevating power, and will find its way into places where naught else will penetrate." The taste for it, when cultivated, by hearing the sublimest compositions the world can boast of, will increase rapidly, and open to many a source of pleasant enjoyment which they never imagined.

We ask the co-operation of those among whom we live,to carry out, to a successful issue, our present plans, and with their aid and countenance, we do not entertain a doubt of the result. We believe the time has now arrived, when the present effort made by the HARMONIA SACRED MUSIC SOCIETY will be a successful one, and that it will become a permanent establishment in this city. We launch our barque upon the waters, and we look to you for encouragement on our voyage. We do it, not in fear and trembling, but with a firm determination to *deserve* success. We can only ask to receive such reward as we merit. We desire no other, and if perseverance and united effort will secure it, we shall have attained our object; "*to advance the cause of music generally, and of sacred music in particular.*"

W. H. W. DARLEY,
*President.*

GEORGE F. JONES,
*Treasurer.*

WILLIAM A. ROLIN,
*Secretary.*

*Philadelphia, October,* 1852.

# AN ACT

## TO INCORPORATE

# THE HARMONIA SACRED MUSIC SOCIETY

### OF PHILADELPHIA.

*Whereas,* Sundry persons in the city and county of Philadelphia, having associated for the purpose of cultivating and improving a taste for Sacred Music, and music generally, and for the better enabling them to accomplish their object and enlarge the beneficial influence of music upon the minds of the citizens: *Therefore*

SECTION 1. *Be it enacted by the Senate and House of Representatives of the Commonwealth of Pennsylvania, in General Assembly met, and it is hereby enacted by the authority of the same:* That William H. W. Darley, George F. Jones, John R. Welsh, John Rutherford, Jr., Thomas M. Davis, Bryant Ferguson, and their associates, members of the association, called the Harmonia Sacred Music Society of Philadelphia, and all such persons as may be hereafter admitted members of the same, shall be and they are hereby constituted and declared to be a body politic and corporate, in deed and in law, by the name, style and title of " *The Harmonia Sacred Music Society of Philadelphia,*" and by the said corporate name shall have perpetual succession, to use a common seal, and to break, alter or renew the same at pleasure, and to take, hold and enjoy lands, tenements and hereditaments, in fee simple, or for any less estate, and personal property, by gift, grant, purchase, devise or bequest, or other lawful means, and sell or dispose of and convey and assign the same, to sue and be sued, and generally to do and perform all such acts, matters and things, as shall be lawful and necessary for them to do to carry out the full and true intent of this act: *Provided*, That the clear annual income of the said society shall not, in any one year, exceed the sum of ten thousand dollars.

SECTION 2. That the essential object of the said Corporation shall be the cultivation of skill and diffusion of taste in music, and the relief of the performing members thereof, in case of sickness, infirmity or other distress, in such manner, and to such extent, as may be determined upon and established in the by-laws of the said society, hereinafter provided for.

SECTION 3. That the officers of said Corporation shall be a President, two Vice-Presidents, a Treasurer, a Secretary and ten Directors, who shall constitute a Board for the transaction of all business of the society, and shall be elected by ballot, by such of the members of the said society as may at the time be entitled under the by-laws to vote at the Annual Meetings of the members, to be held on the Fourth Monday of November in each and every year, forever: *Provided*, That in case an election at any time should not be held at the time appointed therefor, the said society shall not, for that cause, be dissolved, but the election shall be held so soon thereafter as may be, and until such election shall take place, the officers, last chosen, shall continue in the transaction of all business.

SECTION 4. The Treasurer shall hold his office during the pleasure of the Board of Directors, and the books, papers, moneys and accounts in his possession, shall be at all times subject to their inspection and control; he shall give security to the Corporation, to be approved by the Board of Directors, conditioned for the proper performance of his duties, and for the faithful application of all moneys of the society that may come into his hands.

SECTION 5. That the members of said society shall consist of two classes, one thereof to be styled "Performing Members," and the other "Contributing Members."

SECTION 6. The Board of Directors shall have the control over all accounts, moneys and property of the said society, and shall have power to appropriate the funds thereof, in such manner as may to them appear to be most conducive to the interests and objects of the society, and shall have full power to make such by-laws and ordinances as shall and may be deemed necessary to effect the objects of the society, and the same, at any time, to revoke, alter and amend: *Provided*, That such by-laws and ordinances shall not be repugnant to, or inconsistent with the Constitution and laws of this State or of the United States.

SECTION 7. That the Board of Directors shall have power to assess, levy and collect, on and from each and every member of said society, an annual contribution: *Provided*, That the same shall not be less than one dollar, nor greater than ten dollars, and no member of the said society shall be eligible to office, or entitled to vote at any election, nor be entitled to benefits, while he remains in arrears thereof.

SECTION 8. That at every Annual Meeting the Board of Directors shall make a full report of the condition and affairs of the society, and of their proceedings during the time they shall have acted.

SECTION 9. That the character, duties and rights of the several classes of members, the powers and functions of the officers hereinbefore mentioned, and of all those who may be hereafter appointed, the mode of supplying vacancies in office, the times of meeting of the said Corporation, and of the several Boards and Committees respectively, the terms of admission, the mode of proposing and electing members, the causes which shall justify the suspension or disfranchisement of a corporator, and the other concerns of the said Corporation, shall be regulated by the by-laws and ordinances of the same, to be made in pursuance and·by virtue of the power and authority contained and granted in the first section of this act.

SECTION 10. It shall be the duty of the Secretary to give public notice of the time and place of each annual meeting and of the election of officers. The present officers are hereby constituted the officers of the Corporation, and shall continue to hold and exercise their respective offices until the Fourth Monday of November next, and until the officers provided for in this act shall be regularly chosen as aforesaid.

JOHN S. RHEY,
*Speaker of the House of Representatives.*

JOHN H. WALKER,
*Speaker of the Senate.*

Approved the fourth day of May, one thousand eight hundred and fifty-two.

WILLIAM BIGLER.

SECRETARY'S OFFICE,

*Pennsylvania, ss.*

I do hereby certify that the foregoing and annexed is a true and correct copy of the original act of the General Assembly, as the same remains on file in this office.

*In Testimony whereof,* I have hereunto set my hand and caused the seal of the Secretary's Office to be hereunto affixed, at Harrisburg, this thirteenth day of May, A. D. one thousand eight hundred and fifty-two.

E. S. GOODRICH,
*Dep. Secretary of the Commonwealth.*

# BY-LAWS.

## CHAPTER I.

### PRESIDENT.

It shall be the duty of the President to preside at all meetings of the Society and Board of Directors, appoint all committees not appointed by the Board; announce the result of all votes; see that the officers and committees properly perform their duties; enforce an observance of the Constitution, By-Laws and rules of order; vote upon questions when a tie occurs, but not otherwise. It shall be his duty to direct the Secretary to call a special meeting upon application of *five* members of the Society. Special meetings of the Board of Directors shall be subject to the same regulation.

He shall be *ex-officio* member of each Standing Committee.

## CHAPTER II.

### VICE PRESIDENTS.

One of the Vice Presidents shall possess all the powers and perform all the duties of the President whenever he is absent, unable to act, or the office is vacant.

## CHAPTER III.

### TREASURER.

The Treasurer shall receive and receipt for all moneys that may come into his possession, pay all drafts of the Board of Directors, Relief, or other committees authorized to draw from the funds of the Society; report the state of the treasury at every stated meeting of the Board, or at any special meeting when the Board may require, and at the expiration of his official career, he shall hand over the books, papers and funds in his hands, to his successor in office.

## CHAPTER IV.

### SECRETARY.

The Secretary shall, in a book provided for the purpose, fairly and regularly enter all the rules and regulations of the Society, with a register of the names of members.

He shall summon the Board of Directors, and give notice of the meetings of the Society, as may be directed; notify special committees through their chairman; incorporate the reports of the Treasurer and Standing Committees in the minutes.

He shall draft and forward all letters directed to be written by the Board of Directors, and shall preserve copies thereof, which he shall lay before the Board, together with such communications as shall be addressed to him, and shall take charge of all communications addressed to the Society or Board of Directors.

## CHAPTER V.

### BOARD OF DIRECTORS.

SECTION 1. The Board of Directors shall meet on the fourth Monday in February, May, August and November, at such time and place as they may appoint. Seven members shall at all times constitute a quorum.

SECT. 2. Special meetings of the Board may be held at the call of the President, or five members of the Board.

SECT. 3. A majority of the Board shall have power to fill any vacancies that may occur in their body.

SECT. 4. They shall be empowered to apply the funds of the Society for the relief of those performing members who have been regular contributors for two years, who are in any way disabled from pursuing their respective avocations, and shall have discretionary power to extend relief to the widows and children of deceased performing members, *Provided*, That the sum so applied shall not in any one case exceed *fifty dollars*.

SECT. 5. All drafts upon the Treasurer, except those of the Relief Committee, must be made by sanction of the Board of Directors, and no committee except that above named shall be authorized to contract bills or make appropriations until authority has been given them by the Board.

SECT. 6. The annual contribution of each member of the Board shall be *three dollars*, which shall entitle him to all the privileges granted by the Charter and By-Laws.

SECT. 7. The President and Secretary of the Society are *ex-officio* President and Secretary of the Board.

## CHAPTER VI.

### STANDING COMMITTEES.

The following Standing Committees shall be appointed or elected, who may adopt such regulations for their government as may (being in accordance with the Constitution and By-Laws, and subject to the inspection of the Board of Directors,) fully and effectually carry out the objects of their appointment.

### *First—Committee on Music.*

This Committee shall consist of *three.* It shall be their duty to take charge of the musical performances of the Society, under such regulations as the Board of Directors may see fit from time to time to prescribe.

They shall receive applications from persons desirous of becoming performing members, and certify to the Board such as they may approve.

### *Second—Committee on Finance.*

This Committee shall consist of three and the Treasurer "*ex-officio.*" It shall be their duty to devise and report, from time to time, the best practical method for conducting the financial affairs of the Society, and increasing its property.

They shall inspect the accounts of the Treasurer previous to the annual meeting, and report the result of their investigations to the Board of Directors, in time for their action previous to said meeting.

### *Third—Committee of Relief.*

This Committee shall consist of *five,* whose duty it shall be to receive and examine all applications for relief, and when they believe the object worthy and eligible, they shall extend such aid as the necessities of the case may, in their judgment, require: *Provided,* That no applicant shall receive more than *fifty dollars* within any period of twelve months, without special action of the board.

They shall report the result of their operations at every meeting of the Board, and if it should be deemed conducive to the welfare of the Society, they shall present all the attendant circumstances, withholding the name of the applicant, unless called for by a vote.

A majority of the Committee shall have power to act, and their orders on the Treasurer shall be signed by said majority, including the Chairman, or in his absence the Chairman *pro tem.*

## CHAPTER VII.

### REPORTS OF, AND VACANCIES IN COMMITTEES.

SECTION 1. All Committees appointed for special purposes shall report at each stated meeting until discharged.

Sect. 2. No Committee shall be discharged until all bills incurred by it shall have been paid.

Sect. 3. The President shall fill all vacancies that may occur in any Standing or Special Committee, and the Board of Directors shall have power to remove any member of said Committee at their pleasure.

## CHAPTER VIII.
### CHAIRMAN OF COMMITTEES.

Section 1. The first named on a Committee shall act as Chairman thereof until another shall have been chosen, and all reports of Special Committees must be signed by a majority, unless it be a minority report. Reports of Standing Committees may be signed by the Chairman only.

Sect. 2. It shall be the duty of the Chairman of all Committees to call meetings and notify members of the time of assembling.

## CHAPTER IX.
### MEMBERS.

Section 1. The election of members shall be confided to the Board of Directors.

Sect. 2. Every performing member shall pay into the treasury the sum of *two dollars* per annum, and every contributing member shall pay five dollars in like manner—in addition, each performing and contributing member may pay *one dollar* annually into the treasury, which will entitle him (not being in arrears,) to vote at any meeting of the Society.

Sect. 3. Any member of the Society in arrears to the amount of two years contributions, or who refuses to pay the respective contributions, shall be liable to expulsion.

Sect. 4. When a charge shall have been made against any member, and a motion to expel made, such motion shall be referred to the Board of Directors, who *only* shall take action upon it. Notice shall at once be given the member against whom the charge is made, of the existence of such charge, by the Secretary.

Sect. 5. Any member desiring to resign shall signify the wish in writing, addressed to the Board of Directors, and pay all dues, those of the current year inclusive.

Sect. 6. Seven members of the Society, assembled at a special meeting, shall constitute a quorum for the transaction of business.

## CHAPTER X.
### CHANGE OF BY-LAWS.

No alteration or amendment shall be made in these by-laws, unless the same shall have been proposed at a meeting of the Board of Directors one month previous to action being taken.